The Earth Under Sky Bear's Feet

NATIVE AMERICAN POEMS OF THE LAND

Joseph Bruchac · Thomas Locker

PHILOMEL BOOKS

For the children
of all our friends.
—J.B. and T.L.

The Earth Under Sky Bear's Feet

Grandmother sat in front of the lodge. The small girl beside her watched as the old woman's strong hands finished the weaving of the ash splint basket. The glow of the setting sun reflected from the surface of the river, where autumn leaves swirled in the current.

"*Akhsotha*," the girl said, "my grandmother, we must go into the lodge before it is dark. I'm afraid of the night."

Grandmother shook her head, "*Iah*, if we go in too soon, we will not see Sky Bear." Grandmother looked up into the sky, where the pattern of stars that shaped the Great Bear was bright. "Soon she will roam around the skyland."

"Does Sky Bear see everything from up there? Does she hear what we say?"

"*Hen*, Granddaughter, as she travels the sky this whole earth is stretched beneath her feet. Listen, and I will share with you some of the stories our old people tell about what Sky Bear sees and hears through the night."

Sky Bear

Long ago,
three hunters and their little dog
found the tracks of a giant bear.
They followed those tracks
all through the day
and even though it was almost dark
they did not stop, but continued on.
They saw that bear now, climbing up
a hill, which glittered
with new-fallen snow.
They ran hard to catch it,
but the bear was too fast.
They ran and they ran, climbing
up and up until one of the hunters said,
"Brothers, look down."
They did and saw they
were high above Earth.
That bear was Sky Bear,
running on through the stars.
Look up now
and you will see her,
circling the sky.

MOHAWK   Northeast

Song to the Firefly

Beside the great beautiful lake
named Gitchee-gummi,
the sound of voices
drift up into the summer sky,
as the children of the Anishinabe
chase the fireflies,
singing this song.

Small white-fire being,
small white-fire being,
give me light
around my lodge
before I sleep,
before I sleep,
before I sleep — ewee!

Small white-fire being,
small white-fire being,
light my way with your fire,
light my way with your fire,
before I sleep,
before I sleep.

Small white-fire being,
small white-fire being,
let your light
carry me
into sleep.

ANISHINABE   Great Lakes

Flute Song

It is the time
when the rains touch the desert.
All the corn has been planted,
and the flowers blossom.
Now that it is dark,
a young man walks
to the lodge of the girl
who has touched his heart.

Although others may sleep,
now he plays his flute.
Its sweet notes fill the night
and Sky Bear hears
this song
as it lifts to the sky:

Ku-nye-ya ku-hu-na
che-yu-we wa-e-mwe-ta.
I am playing, I am playing
my flute here, and I am shaking,
I am shaking her heart
when the sun goes down.

Ta-sha-e wa-i-ni ke-ma.
When the sun goes down,
I am making, I am making
flowers bloom, and my song
is in her heart.

PIMA   Southwest

Wababanal:
The Northern Lights

Chief Morning Star had an only son;
that boy would not play
with the other children.
Instead, each day
he walked to the north,
and never told anyone where he went.
Night fell and the boy
did not return, so the old chief
followed his son's tracks.

He walked and walked,
and came to a strange land.
The people there wore rainbows as belts.
They had lights on their heads
and played with a ball made of light.
"You are in the land of the Northern
Lights," they said. "Which one
of those boys playing ball is your son?
If you do not know
he can never come home."

Chief Morning Star chose.
"My son," he said, "is that one,
the boy wearing the brightest light."
Two great birds flew down
to carry them home.
Then, all around the father and son,
the *Wa-ba-ba-nal,*
the Northern Lights,
played their game in the sky.

MISSISQUOI   Northeast

Mouse's Bragging Song

In the time when the grass
begins to run green
and the nights grow warm,
the animals wake
from their winter homes.
Sky Bear watches
and smiles as she sees
one family of little mice,
who live beneath a log.
Because they come out at night,
they think they are the only
people in the world.
Just at dusk they come out,
and one little mouse stands on his
hind legs.
He reaches up so high that he
thinks he can touch the sky as he sings:

Moz-hun-nal-ee pe-zhe ya-kis-ke...
On this whole earth
who is there
like me?

Ne-sha-na ma-chi-ni-kgla...
I alone can touch the sky!
Yaki-o-o!
Yaki-o-o!
I alone can touch the sky!

WINNEBAGO   Great Lakes

The Scattered Stars

Why are the stars
scattered all through the sky?
Sky Bear says it happened long ago,
when the people came
from the underworld.
Our Mother, the Mother
of All the People,
gave one little girl named *Ko-tci-man-yo*
a bag made of white cotton
for her to carry.
Do not open this bag, Our Mother said.
But as they walked for many days,
Ko-tci-man-yo felt that bag grow heavy.

One night, when they stopped,
Ko-tci-man-yo climbed up to a hill
where no one could see her,
and then she untied the many knots
to take just one small look inside.
But when she loosened the last knot,
the bag popped open
and bright things began to escape
to the sky.

Ko-tci-man-yo quickly closed that bag,
but only a few of the stars remained
to be placed in patterns in the sky.
All the others scattered.
They are still that way
because of her curiosity.

COCHITI PUEBLO   Southwest

The Seven Mateinnu

Long ago, seven wise men
lived among the people.
They knew so much that everyone
was always asking them for advice.

They grew so tired that
they decided to hide from the people,
and turned themselves
into seven big stones.
But before too long,
the people found them,
and because they were stones,
they had to sit and listen
to everyone ask for help.

They tried a second time to hide,
and turned into seven cedar trees.
But once again,
the people found them,
and because they were rooted,
they still had to listen.

At last they accepted
that they could not hide.
They changed themselves
into seven stars dancing in the middle
of the sky.

Each night the people look up to them
and see the answers to their questions
in the light of those stars.

LENAPE   Eastern Woodlands

The Trail of the Piñon Gatherers

Across the sky
the bright trail of stars stretches.
The Chumash people
know that path
is a cord made of goose down,
which marks the way for the people
on the earth below to follow
north where *piñones* are ripe.
High over that trail
in the middle of the sky
is Sky Coyote,
Star Who Never Moves.
His job is to look after the people.
Each night in the sky
he and Morning Star play *pe-yon*
against Sun and Sky Eagle.
When Sky Coyote
and Morning Star win,
the rains are good
and the people eat well.
As the piñon nut gatherers
walk beneath that great trail,
they sing their thanks
to Sky Coyote and Morning Star
for helping the people.

CHUMASH   West Coast

A Summer Song

Far to the north,
the summer brings
the time of long days
and the midnight sun.
But even though
she cannot be seen,
Sky Bear still circles
and she hears the Inuit people
sing this summer song:

A-ja-ja, it is pleasant,
it is pleasant at last
when the summer comes.

A-ja-ja, it is pleasant,
it is pleasant at last
when the caribou come.

A-ja-ja, they make great noise,
the streams in our country, singing
when the summer comes.

INUIT   Subarctic

The Old Wolf's Song

The wolves have always been great singers.
As Sky Bear watches above the plains
just before the dawn light
touches the earth,
she sees one old wolf
climb the highest hill then lift
his head to sing this song
of his survival to the sky:

An-pa-o can'-na.
At the break of day
I roam

       running

          I roam.

An-pa-o can'-na.
At the break of day
I roam

       trotting

          I roam.

An-pa-o can'-na.
At the break of day
I roam

       in a careful way

          I roam.

An-pa-o can'-na.
At the break of day
I roam

       watching

          I roam.

Into the breath
of another new day

          I roam.

LAKOTA   Great Plains

Dawn House Song

Below the *mesas,*
a new house has been made.
Now as the dawn
starts to brighten the sky,
painting the walls
of the house with light,
Sky Bear hears the people sing:

Far to the east,
there a house was made,
a house was made, a beautiful house.
The Dawn,
there his house was made.
White Corn,
there its house was made.
Soft possessions
for them,
a house was made.
Water in plenty,
for it a house was made.
Corn Pollen,
for it a house was made.

Before me, may it be beautiful.
Behind me, may it be beautiful.
Around me, may it be beautiful.
Below me, may it be beautiful.
Above me, may it be beautiful.
All around me, may it be beautiful.
Within me, may it be beautiful.

NAVAJO   Southwest

Spirit Dance Song

The spirit dancers gathered
at sundown to dance,
and this is the song
that Sky Bear
heard them sing,
until the rising
of the Morning Star:

Ru-we-re-ra, ru-we-re-ra.
Look where she comes,
The Evening Star.

Re-ra-wha-a, re-ra-wha-a.
Many are coming,
The stars of the skyland.

Ru-we-re-ra, ru-we-re-ra.
Look where she comes,
Mother Moon, Mother Moon.

Ru-we-re-ra, ru-we-re-ra.
Look where he comes,
the Star of Morning.

Ru-we-re-ra, ru-we-re-ra.
Look where he comes,
Father Sun, Father Sun.

PAWNEE   Great Plains

Author's Note

Although they speak hundreds of different languages, the Native peoples of North America all share an awareness that the world around them is very much alive. I remember an Iroquois elder telling me many years ago that everything in nature has its own voice and its own story. Often, those voices and stories can be found in songs still sung in honor of the natural world that contemporary Americans too often ignore—from the tiny mouse reaching up to the sky to the awesome flow of color across the heavens that is the Northern Lights.

One wonderful story, which is found where I grew up in the northeastern corner of North America, tells how the pattern of stars known by many as the Big Dipper is actually a great bear circling the night. Thinking of what that great bear might see, as the land and the seasons change, was the start of this collection, but the traditional Native American songs and stories that I drew upon are what gave Sky Bear's vision life. I wanted to remind readers that, as Native children have always been taught, there can be as much to see in the living night as in the more familiar light of day.

The Iroquois grandmother who tells these tales is very much like a good friend of mine, Marion Miller, a traditional Seneca storyteller who fascinates children and grown-ups alike with her stories about the stars. I hope that, as I do, you will hear her voice and the gentle voices of the many elders who have shared with us their stories and their songs of a night that is not to be feared.

Joseph Bruchac